FEB 1 0

REMARKABLE
CANADIANS

Don
Cherry

by Tina
Schwartzenberger

Published by Weigl Educational Publishers Limited
6325 10 Street SE
Calgary, Alberta, Canada
T2H 2Z9

Website: www.weigl.com
Copyright ©2009 Weigl Educational Publishers Limited

All of the Internet URLs given in the book were valid at the time of publication.
However, due to the dynamic nature of the Internet, some addresses may have
changed, or sites may have ceased to exist since publication. While the author and
publisher regret any inconvenience this may cause readers, no responsibility for any
such changes can be accepted by either the author or the publisher.

Library and Archives Canada Cataloguing in Publication data available upon request.
Fax (403) 233-7769 for the attention of the Publishing Records department.

ISBN 978-1-55388-458-3 (hard cover)
ISBN 978-1-55388-459-0 (soft cover)

Printed in the United States of America
1 2 3 4 5 6 7 8 9 0 12 11 10 09 08

Editor: Heather C. Hudak
Design: Terry Paulhus

Photograph Credits
Weigl acknowledges Getty Images as the primary image supplier for this title.
International Hockey Hall of Fame: page 7 bottom left. Sportsnet: page 13 top right.

Every reasonable effort has been made to trace ownership and to obtain
permission to reprint copyright material. The publishers would be pleased
to have any errors or omissions brought to their attention so that they may
be corrected in subsequent printings.

We gratefully acknowledge the financial support of the Government of Canada
through the Book Publishing Industry Development Program (BPIDP) for our
publishing activities.

Contents

Who Is Don Cherry?

From October through June, nearly 1.5 million Canadians watch Don Cherry every Saturday night. Don co-hosts "Coach's Corner," a popular program on the television show *Hockey Night in Canada*. Don loves hockey. He was a hockey player and a coach before he joined "Coach's Corner." He also has been a hockey team manager and owner. Don uses his television program to share his love of the sport and his opinions about the game. Don has done a great deal to promote the sport of hockey in Canada. He often gives advice to young hockey players and helps with many charity events.

> "I don't have any hobbies. I don't golf. I don't fish. I have no other interests in life except hockey. I wake up in the morning thinking about it and go to bed thinking about it."

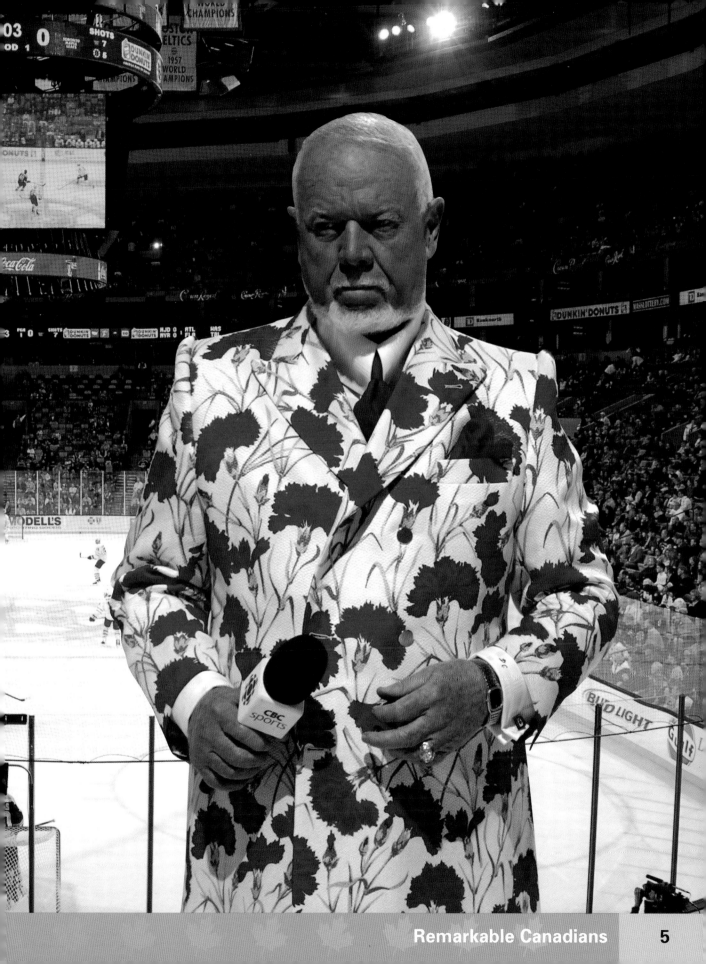

Growing Up

Donald Stewart Cherry was born in Kingston, Ontario, on February 5, 1934. His mother, Maude, taught him to stand up for himself. His father, Del, was an electrician and **amateur** baseball player. He read Don stories about successful people.

Don grew up playing hockey. He was a small boy, but he played the game well. He played **defense** for the Windsor Spitfires and Barrie Flyers as a teenager.

Don wanted to be a police officer when he was young. Today, he uses his television show to honour police officers, firefighters, and soldiers who have died doing their jobs.

The Spitfires are a junior hockey team that plays in the Ontario Hockey League.

Ontario Tidbits

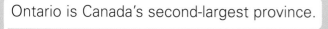

BIRD
Common
Loon

TREE
Eastern
White Pine

FLOWER
White
Trillium

Ontario is Canada's second-largest province.

Ontario contains about one-third of the world's fresh water.

The highest point in Ontario is the Timiskaming district, which rises 693 metres above sea level.

More than 12 million people live in the province of Ontario.

Toronto is Ontario's capital city. Ottawa, the capital city of Canada, also is in Ontario.

Think about it!

Kingston is sometimes called the "birthplace of hockey." It is home to the International Hockey Hall of Fame, and many hockey players have come from this city. How do you think growing up in Kingston might have influenced Don? Think about the place where you live. What is special about your community? How has this influenced you?

Practice Makes Perfect

At age 14, Don left school to play hockey full time. In 1954, he signed a **contract** to play with the American Hockey League Hershey Bears in Hershey, Pennsylvania. That year, Don met Rosemarie Martini and asked her on a date. On their first date, he took her to a hockey game that he was playing in. Two years later, they were married. For the next 16 years, Don played hockey as a professional minor league defenseman with many teams in Canada and the United States. During that time, Don and Rosemarie had two children, Cindy and Tim.

The Hershey Bears joined the AHL in 1938. They have played more than 5,000 games.

In 1970, Don retired from hockey. He tried many different jobs to earn money so that he could provide for his wife and children. For a while, Don worked as a luxury car salesman. Later, he took a job working in construction.

Don missed hockey and returned to the game in 1971. He signed with the Rochester Americans. Don rarely played. Midway through the season, the owners asked Don to take over as coach. Don did such a good job that he was offered the job of coach for the 1972 to 1973 season.

🍁 In addition to the Hershey Bears, Don played in the AHL with the Rochester Americans and the Springfield Indians.

Key Events

After three years coaching in the AHL, in 1974, Don became coach of the NHL's Boston Bruins. Don received the Jack Adams Award for coach of the year for the 1975 to 1976 season. He also was chosen as an assistant coach in the 1976 Canada Cup.

In 1979, Don's hockey career came to a sudden end. The Bruins received a **penalty** for too many men on the ice in game seven of the Stanley Cup final. There were fewer than two minutes left in the game. Montreal tied the game and went on to win in **overtime**. The general manager of the Bruins, Harry Sinden, fired Don. After the Boston Bruins fired Don, he coached the Colorado Rockies during the 1979 to 1980 season. They finished in last place. In spring 1980, Don was fired as coach.

One night in 1980, Don appeared on the *Hockey Night in Canada* television program. Canadian Broadcasting Corporation (CBC) officials were so impressed with Don that they created a **segment** for him on the show called "Coach's Corner." It airs after the first period of the hockey game ends.

With Don as coach, the Bruins won four division titles in a row. They lost to the Montreal Canadiens in the 1977 and 1978 Stanley Cup finals.

Thoughts from Don

Don is well-known for saying what is on his mind. People do not always agree with what he says.

Don recalls his first time coaching hockey.

"As soon as I got behind the bench, I knew I was born for it."

Don remembers his dad.

"I get chills describing him. I was proud walking down the street with him. You knew he was somebody; he turned heads."

Don remembers his mom helping him when he played hockey.

"I remember I was going away to Barrie (to play with the Flyers) and we had old gloves with holes. I remember my mother going and getting me new gloves. I was the only one with new gloves."

Don talks about his favorite player.

"I coached Bobby Orr, the greatest player ever. And he had his greatest year, I thought, with me."

Growing up, Don always dreamed of playing hockey.

"I prayed every night I'd be hockey player. I guess I just forgot to mention to the Lord I wanted to play in the National Hockey League."

Don talks about being on television.

"When you start thinking you're a somebody for being on television, you are in deep trouble."

Don is always willing to share his opinion.

"I know exactly what I'm saying, so that when I'm fired, it won't be a slip of the tongue. Everything I want to say I say."

What Is a Sportscaster?

Sportscasters are people who report about sporting events on television or on the radio. As the game is being played, sportscasters provide details about the live action and the players. There are two types of sportscasters, play-by-play announcers and colour **commentators**. A play-by-play announcer will often have formal training as a reporter. This person knows a great deal about many types of sports. The colour commentator is usually someone who has a great deal of knowledge about a certain sport. This person may have played or coached the sport. He or she can provide stories about the players and inside information about the game. On most sports programs, there is both a play-by-play announcer and a colour commentator.

Don Cherry played hockey for many years. He passed his knowledge of the sport on to the players he coached. Today, Don shares his knowledge and opinions about hockey with people who watch "Coach's Corner."

Don is a colour commentator. He also provides game analysis.

Sportscasters 101

Ron MacLean (1960–)

Position Host

Achievements Ron MacLean has been working as a broadcaster since 1978. He worked on a number of television and radio programs before joining *Hockey Night in Canada* in 1986. At first, Ron was hired to cover games in western Canada. By the end of his first season with the show, he had moved to Toronto and had **anchored** the Stanley Cup playoffs. Since then, he has been the main host of the show. Ron co-hosts "Coach's Corner" with Don Cherry. In addition to *Hockey Night in Canada*, Ron has hosted major world sporting events, including the Olympics for the CBC. He has won many awards recognizing excellence in Canadian television broadcasting.

Martine Gaillard (1971–)

Position Co-Anchor

Achievements As a child, Martine Gaillard played all types of sports. She decided at a young age that she wanted to work in television, interviewing athletes. After high school, Martine went to college in Saskatoon. Then, she attended Ryerson University in Toronto to obtain a degree in the radio and television arts. Her first job in sports broadcasting was as a game host for the Toronto Maple Leafs. After two years, Martine took a job with a sports news network called *The Score*. She was the first woman to anchor a show on the network. Later, Martine worked on *Hockey Night in Canada*. In 2005, she took a job as with Rogers Sportsnet, a television channel that airs only sports-related programs. Today, she continues to work for this channel as a co-anchor with Mike Roth on *SportsnetNews*.

Don Wittman

Position Anchor

Achievements Don Wittman was one of the Canada's best-known sportscasters until his death in 2008. After graduating from the University of Saskatchewan, Don took his first job as a radio host in 1955. He went on to host radio and television programs about all types of sports, including baseball, hockey, basketball, curling, and golf. Over a career that spanned nearly 50 years, Don won numerous awards for his work, such as Sports Media Canada Broadcaster of the Year. In January 2008, he was inducted into the CBC Sports Hall of Fame.

Kelly Hrudey (1961–)

Position Anchor

Achievements For 15 years, Kelly Hrudey was a goaltender in the NHL. In 1998, he retired from the game and became a sportscaster with *Hockey Night in Canada*. Hrudey uses his experience as a hockey player to provide insight into the game. He has hosted many segments on *Hockey Night in Canada*, including "After Hours" and "Behind the Mask." When Hrudey is not working with the CBC, he works on other radio and television programs and writes a column with the *Calgary Sun*.

Television
The first television broadcasts took place in Great Britain in the mid-1930s. Broadcasts soon took place in the United States but were put on hold until after World War II ended. Following the war, black-and-white televisions became widely available. Colour televisions first debuted in the 1950s. Today, most North Americans have at least one television in their home.

Influences

As a coach, Don Cherry became known for his unusual clothing. He is known for wearing **double-breasted** suits that are often brightly coloured and have large patterns. He also wears cuff links, gloves, and hats. Don's sense of style was influenced by his father, Del. Del wore three-piece suits, dressy hats, and a gold watch. Don has said that people admired the way his father dressed.

Many of Don Cherry's clothes are custom made.

Don was also known for his actions on the bench. As a coach, Don studied historic military leaders, such as Lord Horatio Nelson and Sir Francis Drake. From these leaders, Don learned how to treat people. He has said that a team is like a ship and that everybody has to pull together to accomplish a task.

🐾 The Boston Bruins players gave Don an English bull terrier dog that he named Blue. Blue died in 1989, but Don got another English bull terrier that he also named Blue.

THE NATIONAL HOCKEY LEAGUE

The National Hockey League was established in Montreal in November 1917. There were five original teams. These were the Montreal Canadiens, Quebec Bulldogs, Montreal Wanderers, Ottawa Senators, and Toronto Arenas. In 1924, the Boston Bruins became the first American team to join the NHL. Today, there are 30 teams in the NHL.

Overcoming Obstacles

While Don was coaching the Boston Bruins, his son, Tim, became very ill. Tim developed kidney disease when he was 13 years old. Tim had dialysis treatment for months. Dialysis is a medical process that cleans a patient's blood using a special machine. In healthy people, the kidneys perform this function.

Over time, Tim became quite ill, and he needed a kidney transplant. This is a major operation, and Don feared Tim would not survive. Don, Rose, and Cindy were all tested to see if one of them could donate a kidney to Tim. Cindy was found to be a match. She donated one of her kidneys to her brother. Today, Don is a spokesperson for organ donation awareness. He wants people to know that they can donate organs to family members and other sick people.

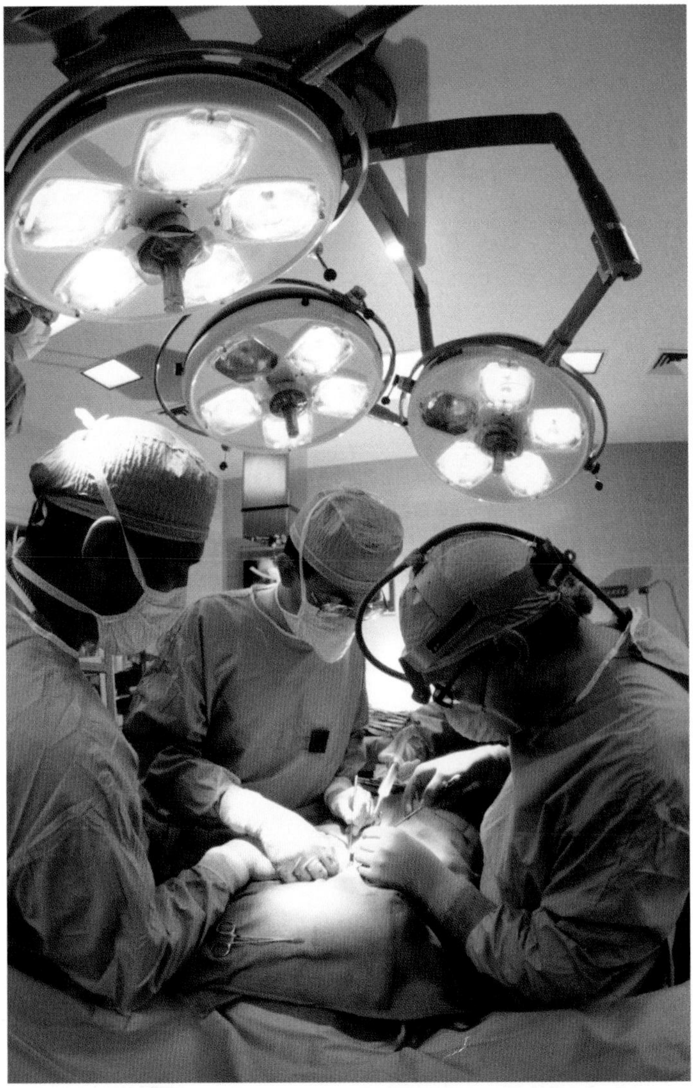

During a kidney transplant, doctors remove unhealthy kidneys from a patient and replace them with a healthy one that is taken from another person.

Don's wife Rose died of cancer in 1997. This was a difficult time for Don, and he felt very lonely. He and Rose had been married for 40 years. She had been Don's **agent**, manager, secretary, and personal banker. Rose was the love of his life and a dear friend. Then, Don met a woman named Luba at a hockey event. The two later married.

Don returned to minor hockey in 1998. He joined with three **investors** to create the Mississauga Ice Dogs, a team in the Ontario Hockey League. In the 2000 to 2001 season, the Ice Dogs won only 3 of 68 games. The investors were disappointed. In September 2001, Don took over as head coach of the team for one season. They improved only slightly, winning 11 games. Don did not give up hope. The following year, another coach took over, and the team made it to the playoffs. Don sold the team in 2006.

Sometimes, other people do not like Don's comments. However, he knows there are many people who value his thoughts.

Achievements and Successes

Don was a successful coach. Under Don, the Boston Bruins finished first in their division four seasons in a row. He was voted coach of the year and coached Team Canada in 1976. He won 250 games in fewer games than any other coach in the NHL.

In 2005, Don Cherry's team won the Top Prospects game at the Pacific Coliseum in Vancouver, British Columbia.

In 2004, the CBC held a contest to find out who Canadians thought was the "greatest" Canadian. They asked citizens to nominate people they felt were worthy of this title. Don Cherry ranked number seven out of 100 nominees.

Today, Don Cherry is one of the best-known celebrities in Canada. He has hosted radio shows, made videos about great moments in hockey, starred in commercials, and even opened a chain of restaurants. "Coach's Corner" remains one of the top-rated Canadian television shows.

GIVING BACK TO THE COMMUNITY: ROSE CHERRY'S HOME FOR KIDS

After Rose died, her family wanted to do something in her memory. They decided to create Rose Cherry's Home for Kids. In 2003, Don began raising money for Rose Cherry's Home for Kids. This **hospice** for terminally ill children is located in Milton, Ontario. The centre opened in September 2004 and is now called the Darling Home for Kids. The home includes a snoezelen room, which is a space where soothing music is played, lights shift, and gentle breezes blow. This room is comforting for sick children. To learn more about the Darling Home for Kids, visit **www.darlinghomeforkids.ca**.

Write a Biography

A person's life story can be the subject of a book. This kind of book is called a biography. Biographies describe the lives of remarkable people, such as those who have achieved great success or have done important things to help others. These people may be alive today, or they may have lived many years ago. Reading a biography can help you learn more about a remarkable person.

At school, you might be asked to write a biography. First, decide who you want to write about. You can choose a sportscaster, such as Don Cherry, or any other person you find interesting. Then, find out if your library has any books about this person. Learn as much as you can about him or her. Write down the key events in this person's life. What was this person's childhood like? What has he or she accomplished? What are his or her goals? What makes this person special or unusual?

A concept web is a useful research tool. Read the questions in the following concept web. Answer the questions in your notebook. Your answers will help you write your biography review.

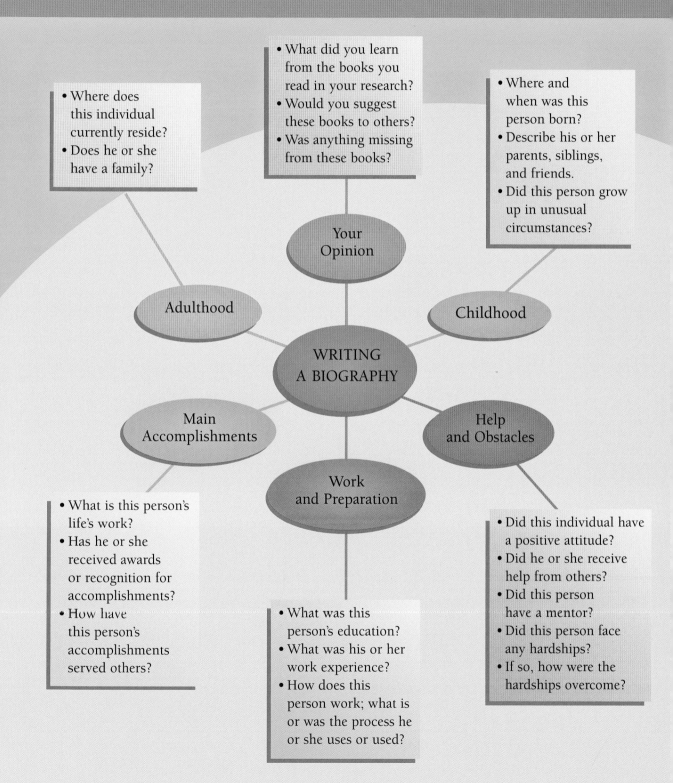

- Where does this individual currently reside?
- Does he or she have a family?

- What did you learn from the books you read in your research?
- Would you suggest these books to others?
- Was anything missing from these books?

- Where and when was this person born?
- Describe his or her parents, siblings, and friends.
- Did this person grow up in unusual circumstances?

Your Opinion

Adulthood

Childhood

WRITING A BIOGRAPHY

Main Accomplishments

Help and Obstacles

Work and Preparation

- What is this person's life's work?
- Has he or she received awards or recognition for accomplishments?
- How have this person's accomplishments served others?

- What was this person's education?
- What was his or her work experience?
- How does this person work; what is or was the process he or she uses or used?

- Did this individual have a positive attitude?
- Did he or she receive help from others?
- Did this person have a mentor?
- Did this person face any hardships?
- If so, how were the hardships overcome?

Timeline

YEAR	DON CHERRY	WORLD EVENTS
1930s	Don Cherry is born on February 5, 1934 in Kingston, Ontario.	In 1938, the first NHL **exhibition games** are played in Europe, between Montreal and Detroit.
1950s	Don plays the only NHL game of his career for the Boston Bruins in 1955.	The USSR becomes a member of the International Ice Hockey Federation in 1953.
1970s	Don returns to hockey in 1971, playing for the Rochester Americans.	In 1970, the Boston Bruins win the Stanley Cup for the first time in 29 years. They win again two years later.
1990s	Don's wife Rose dies in 1997.	Women's ice hockey becomes an Olympic sport at the 1998 Winter Olympics in Nagano, Japan.
2000s	In 2005, Don is made an honourary member of the Police Association of Ontario.	In 2004, an NHL strike keeps players from taking to the ice for an entire season.

Further Research

How can I find out more about Sidney Crosby?

Most libraries have computers that connect to a database that contains information on books and articles about different subjects. You can input a key word and find material on that person, place, or thing you want to learn more about. The computer will provide you with a list of books in the library that contain information on the subject you searched for. Non-fiction books are arranged numerically, using their call number. Fiction books are organized alphabetically by the author's last name.

Websites

To learn more about Don Cherry, visit www.legendsofhockey.net, and search for Don Cherry.

To see a list of the top 10 Greatest Canadians, including Don Cherry, visit www.cbc.ca/greatest/top_ten

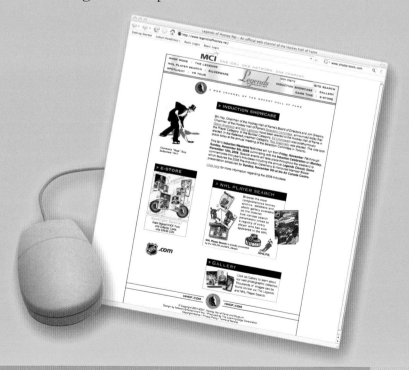

Words to Know

agent: someone who represents an athlete and helps them get the best salary or find the team that best suits the player

amateur: a person who is not paid to take part in a sport

anchored: acted as host for a television or radio show

commentators: people who report on and analyze events

contract: a written agreement between a hockey player and a team that states how long the player will play for the team for and how much the team will pay the player

defense: a hockey player who helps stop the opposing team from scoring points on goal

double-breasted: to have a great deal of fabric in the front and an extra row of buttons

exhibition games: games played outside of the regular hockey season; regular rules apply, but the game does not count for points in the season

hospice: a place that provides medical care to people who are extremely ill

investors: people who put their money toward a cause or goal

overtime: time added to a sporting event to break a tie after the regular play has ended

penalty: to sit out of the game for a certain period of time after breaking a rule

segment: part of a television program

Index